I0467574

The
Seven Step
Rocket
Start-Up Plan:
Your Hard Truth Cheat Sheet
for Starting Your Own
Successful Small Business

Alan Kerrman
Notable Media

ISBN-13: 978-1533344991
ISBN-10: 153334499X

First Edition, v. 1.2
Published by NOTABLE MEDIA

For my darling wife and our hilarious daughter, you're the best -- even though sometimes you're both so loud I can barely get any work done!

Also by Alan Kerrman:

Trading Options on Tech Stocks

Investing in DRIPs

(also available in audiobook)

Preface

Start-Ups and Small Businesses Need to
Launch the Right Way

*I've launched (and helped create!)
several small businesses, and I've made
every mistake that you can make. I
have written this for those
entrepreneurs, founders, or small
business types who are in "knowledge-
input-mode" where they want to learn
from the best-practices, avoidable
mistakes -- and the occasional wisdom
-- of others.*

*Here's your seven step start-up
plan that will fit small businesses of all
types: products or services, web-based*

or offline. Let's talk about money, revenues, sales, partners, co-founders, web 3.0, and more, in a no-nonsense, cheat-sheet guide to getting you launched fast! Here's a start-up plan that will fit small businesses and new businesses of all types. Let's talk about money, revenues, sales, partners, co-founders, web 3.0, and more, in a no-nonsense, cheat-sheet guide to getting you LAUNCHED!

Introduction

First, thanks for reading my new book: the **Seven Step Rocket Start-Up Plan**! Congratulations on moving forward with your own business or business idea and best of luck with the initial stages. Launching your start-up is fun and exciting, but it's also a challenging and critical time for you! I'm not your standard business consultant-type, so I apprcciatc you taking the time to check out this short book! I promise that you'll get some actionable goodies here, so let's get started!

Yes, this is meant to be a quick read so you can get back to the matter at hand. And since this is a "concise" book about your new small business launch, I don't want to pull any punches. What you need is the truth.

Most small businesses fail. Why? Well, not because the founders/owners and proprietors are the wrong people to start them. Not because the ideas for the company weren't robust enough, although that does happen. Not because customers and clients aren't out there waiting for your product or service. Nope.

I think most small business fail at the *execution* stage. Can you -- and your partners or co-founders -- actually launch this business? Can you run it? Can you make the right decisions at the right time? Can you maintain your priorities and manage growth?

I wrote this because I'm aiming to give you some real, get-started-now tips in these pages, but we also need you to get focused on the right things. Why? If you're starting a business now, you don't have time to read about all the different possibilities! You need just to launch into action.

Personally, I've always liked the image of a rocket for business because we do a certain amount of preparations, plan for all contingencies, and then aim for the sky and launch. LAUNCH. As the founder, president, or proprietor of your new business, you need to get immediately moving with your idea. You need to go fast to get some traction with your company, build some momentum, and take off. (Escape velocity!) That's why the perfect image for this stage of your idea and your growth is the rocket or space shuttle!

The start-up process is fun, exhilarating, scary, and more, but it can also be confusing, especially if you've spent most of your career working for someone else. But even if you are an entrepreneur at heart, you might second-guess yourself when it comes to your great small business idea.

WHY DID I WRITE THIS PLAN?

I think people need a quick recipe or a checklist, or a plan of attack -- even if they already know what steps they'll take. It's essentially for confirmation so that when you see what I've laid out, you can immediately get started, or tweak the steps or order once you know what you've got to do. So I give you seven (7)-- count 'em SEVEN steps, and with this have created my Seven-Step Rocket Start-Up Plan, perfect for small businesses with either a service or a product launch.

Okay, so why did I write this?

A friend, former co-worker, and a colleague met with me over lunch a few months ago and asked me to help him get his floundering business IDEA off the ground. He knew I had created a successful small business of my own, and that I was making new web businesses, finding new joint ventures, launching some private label products, and more.

I was very enthusiastic about helping him with his initial stage questions. I truly love this kind of stuff -- my brain is hardwired for this type of big-picture thinking, and I like pointing my entrepreneurial passions at a new project! I was excited for him and the new chapter in his personal and professional life, and I was excited to help him implement some of the strategies, steps, and organizational ideas that I know would work.

What he told me is that he has actually been working part-time at this business for a while, but his plans on how to structure it into a full-fledged, full-time company had stumbled, and he had been treading water for two years. I was even more intrigued!

Personally, I felt that he had a great business idea, and one that would work in our regional marketplace. He was planning to launch a service business in a rather wealthy area -- and a vacation hotspot -- so he had the benefit of good year-round clients and the possibility of a new wave of customers every tourist season. And because it was a niche business with a serious barrier to entry for others, I knew it was possible for my friend to convert this into a full-time business in a very short amount of time. (He was qualified to do this type of work while his competitors may not be.) And based on what he told me, a transition to full-time would be GREAT.

Does any of this story sound familiar yet?

This start-up guy and his brother, who come from a strict working-class family, were the first in their entire family to go to college. But he believed that college was the answer to everything. He started a community college, transferred to a 4-year college and earned a bachelor's degree. Not bad! Then he found an opportunity to pursue a grad program in a neighboring state and after two more years received a master's degree. Amazing, right?

Yes, but the degree is a niche and one where it's hard to make a living even in a great economy. So now from pursuing this family dream of higher education, he has ridiculous student loans for his undergrad and grad school studies in excess of $90,000! I was floored! When he told me the amount of all his monthly bills, including these loans, running his own business was probably the BEST way to clear this debt and get on with his life! If he owned something and worked hard, he wouldn't have the salary cap of a regular job.

HELPING HIS SERVICE BUSINESS START-UP

So we got started, and I jumped in 150%! I had his company's PHASE ONE game plan partially crafted on my drive home from that first meeting. But I found out rather quickly that I was the only one ROWING that boat! My friend was clearly still in his part-time, slow motion mode and seemed almost incapable of making any quick decisions.

Logo, website, company name, branding? Sorry, founders but you have some decisions to make! I created an action plan for him that included new branding, immediate regional and national level (cheap!) marketing, the launch of a new website, and a task list

15

for the first phase of his new start-up. (I told him it was better just to assume that we were now starting from scratch!)

We would meet, usually at coffee shops or libraries, to discuss plans, direct and finances. He was all talk about the future and earnings potential, and the prestige of an established company, but didn't see that immediate steps right in front of him. I wanted to be an inspiring consultant and help him efficiently launch, and what I found was that he wanted me to do all the work, maybe even become a partner. (Good business idea, but not what I wanted to spend my energy on.)

As you can imagine, we had a rough collaboration, and I learned some very precious lessons. He often told me that he felt like I was rushing him to make a decision, and in many ways, I think it's a stylistic difference. I was rushing him! You can always change the logo later, or even rebrand the company, but if you don't start, you can't even get any market or customer feedback. If you don't have a product or service available, then you have no customers or clients, and you have no business.

I'm not saying that rockets should launch in Florida without a lot of pre-flight work in Houston (yes, another NASA reference). But a countdown to launch that goes forever never tests whether your idea can fly. I'd rather start fast and fail fast and move on to my next idea than poke around for three years only to find out that nobody wants my product or service. The founder/chief/president/owner/proprietor needs to know what to do, what they want to do, and how to TAKE DEFINITIVE ACTION. Otherwise, there is no business. Period.

The short version is that I helped this guy as much as I could. And as a friend and a client, I essentially told him to un-hire me, and not to call me about this project unless he was ready to move forward. (Another year has gone by for him.) He's one of those people who, unfortunately, has a decent small business idea, but refuses to take the right steps to get off the ground. Perhaps he can read this book too, and see how easy it is to LAUNCH!

These are the action steps I told him that he should make, and now you can use them to launch your small business.

So let's get started.

Step One - Launch

ACTUALLY Launch!

The most important thing you can do for your business is just get started. Just launch. Stop thinking about it, talking about it, and move forward.

It seems like an obvious step, but you'd be surprised how many people have a business idea, and never actually take any real action. Don't be one of them. Here's a simple digital questionnaire that will make you realize if you're moving or not.

Answer these questions (on a separate sheet of paper, or in your head, if you prefer):

- When did/will you start your business? _ _ - _ _ - _ _ _ _ (Exact date format: MM-DD-YYYY)
- Do you know your business structure: sole proprietorship, partnership, LLC, or corporation? *YES or NO*
- Do you have a company name? *YES or NO*
- Did you already get a business certificate from your city or town hall? *YES or NO*
- Do you plan to use your home address for your company, or do you need a post office mailbox address? *YES or NO*
- Do you have a separate checking account (and money

market savings) for this company? *YES or NO*

- Do you have a dedicated telephone number you can use with your business? Will you use your personal cell phone/wireless? *YES or NO*

- Do you have a logo, image, slogan, business motto, and mission statement? *YES or NO*

- Do you have a simple, professional website for your business on the web? *YES or NO*

There's the entire PHASE ONE part of launching your small business. And the most amazing part of this and that you can complete most of those tasks in a single day!

Here's a hypothetical example:

9 AM -- I decide that I will be launching my new business *today*. In this example, I've decided I'm going to start a company to do landscape design consulting in my area. I decide that I will begin as a sole proprietor (or a DBA "doing business as", in my state) and that if I decide to incorporate, I'll deal with that later.

10 AM - I decide to call my (imaginary) company SHRUBS BY ALAN, and I head off to my local town/ city hall to get a business certificate. In my state and town, I fill it out as Alan Kerrman d/b/a ("doing business as") SHRUBS BY ALAN, and choose "sole proprietorship" for the business structure. Remember, if I want I can always incorporate later (as an LLC, C Corp, S Corp, Partnership, etc.) For reasons of commercial vs. residential zoning, they will ask me about company operations, and I tell them that while I'll operate out of my home only the telephone/computer, all of the service work is done on location at a client's residence or business.

For a product business, unless you're hoping to open a retail location, all of your sales can take place online, at trade shows, flea markets, etc, and customers will not come to your business location. I'll pay the small annual registration fee for the business certificate (varies), and be on my way. (Here it's about $50 per year.)

11 AM - I'm not sure that my home would ever be confused with a landscaping and garden center, but I still want the "official" address of the company to be a P.O. Box or Mail Box location in town. This separate address is also useful if there's a chance we'll move within a couple years. (You don't want work-related checks subject to any mail-forwarding issues.) Home addresses for companies like this might encourage some customers just to show up.

If I'm at the Post Office, I'm filling out the paperwork with my name and my company name (show them your business certificate!), and paying for a small mailbox -- either with six-month or annual rent. Save your money -- don't rent the largest box size, unless it makes some sense for your business.

12 PM - A quick lunch, and then off to the bank with your business certificate and P.O. Box address. What you need is to open a business checking account in the company name. (You'll probably need a small deposit - either cash or a check written out to your new company or you individually. One hundred to five hundred dollars ($100 - $500) is a good start - but ask your bank what they need.) If this is already your primary bank, your new accounts can be linked to your personal checking for easy transfers. The checks will show either the company and P.O. Box address, or Alan Kerrman d/b/a Shrubs by Alan and then the address. Leave your telephone number off your printed checks unless you have a logical reason to include them. I get starter checks, and a small batch of printed checks are on the way. If I want a business logo on the checks later, I'll do that with my first re-order.

1 PM - I decide that I'll get a new separate cell phone for my business. I can either request another line on my current plan or stop by an area wireless telephone stores. Keeping costs down, I choose an earlier generation refurbished smartphone of some sort. This separate device will help me check email, and be accessible while I'm on the go, but will dedicate a specific number (and voicemail) for the business. With the wireless carrier, I try to select a new telephone number in an exchange and area code that makes sense for my business. (For example, my business cell has a number from a city north of here that is considered more upscale. It was a lucky accident but has helped with a few clients.) If a separate phone isn't necessary, consider adding a unique voicemail number for incoming calls. Google Voice is one possibility, as is a nationwide toll-free number from companies like Grasshopper.com, and others.

2 PM - Back home by mid-afternoon and I decide to research getting a logo and a website for my company. Search online for web developers in your area, or get a domain name and shared Wordpress hosting and do it yourself. Try to avoid launching any commercial business on a free Wordpress, Wix, or Blogspot site, because some clients will be "turned off" before they even connect with you. If you don't have the skills yourself, there are sites like 99Designs, Upwork, Freelancer, Fiverr, and others where you can hire domestic or international graphic designers and web developers to create your basic branding. With 99Designs, plan on spending a few hundred dollars to get a couple dozen high-end logo samples from designers angling for your business. Once you have a great company logo, it becomes easier later to promote the business because it just looks professional -- you'll never have to apologize for it being less than perfect. Place your orders for a site and a logo, and you could have everything delivered in a few days to a week.

You are launched!

Even though I'm basing this list on an imaginary launch, I've done many of these steps for past start-ups in a single day. My warning to you is that I also know some "wantrepreneurs" who haven't taken these steps although they've been talking about starting their business idea for months. Your particular jurisdiction and/or situation might require a few more steps, or incur some administrative delays (getting a state tax-exempt resale certificate, for example), but you get the general idea of what can be accomplished and how quickly.

Step Two - The Web

REALIZE That Your Website Is Not Your Business - Represent Yourself.

Many years ago, can you imagine that businesses had to be encouraged even to have a website. Of course, it's easy to forget that the web is less than 30 years old (yeah, the '90s!). But now we have the opposite problem. Some people launch a simple website, sometimes even just a single landing page, and assume they've started their business.

Of course, some websites are massive companies and businesses. Sure my dripinvestingplans.com site is a simple blog about personal finance, but Yahoo.com is a $38 billion dollar market cap global corporation. But unless your business is web-only, you'll need to represent the business yourself. Web 2.0 and 3.0 technology doesn't replace personal connections, new contents, meeting people in person, or having a positive telephone or video chat conversation.

Think about what aspects of your company are truly helped by the power of the web -- and by having your website -- but also plan those opportunities for growth that come from networking events, visiting prospects, trade shows, sponsorships, or other activities that can't be accomplished online. Although it seems like a quaint, almost dated concept -- attending a business after-hours event sponsored by your local chamber of commerce, incubator, VCs, or co-working space, is a great way to meet other business people in your area who could become your suppliers, your subcontractors, or even your customers.

[Image: social-371649.png]

Imagine that you're up and running, your business is alive and prospering, and you've already started your company website. Maybe you even created a business Facebook page, a Twitter account, and a YouTube channel. Awesome! But that can't take away from the fact that this business is actually you (and your co-founders), and whether or not you want to stay behind the scenes, you need to be the *face* of your company -- at least for now. Even if your business is entirely online (as a product or service), you must realize that your website, your LinkedIn profile,

Facebook business page, YouTube Channel, or your overall online presence as a company is NOT your business. You are.

Step Three - Money

CONCENTRATE On The Money Coming
In - Booking Work, Making Sales,
Generating Revenues, and developing
Cash Flow!

Focusing immediately on revenue
and income is pretty solid, well-known
advice, but it cannot be stressed enough.
Concentrate now on bringing money
into your business. Make your first sale,
book your first client, even pre-sell your
products. If you get revenues and cash
flow working from the beginning, then
you're more likely to succeed in your
new start-up. You'll be able to pay your
bills and reinvest in your business
without continually racking up personal
or business debt to get your idea off the

ground. You've heard the expression that "Cash is King," well, I think it should be "Cash Flow is King!"

There are statistics online about the number of small businesses that fail within the first couple years, and the percentage is incredibly high. Scary high. But that's okay because if you make money, make a sale, have revenue in the first couple months of running your business, the percentage of failure drops a lot. That alone should motivate you to start with income.

Why do so many people do the opposite? Many entrepreneurs and new business owners are so concerned with the perception of their company that they'll spend all sorts of money on business cards, websites, domain names, logo design, office space, office equipment, consulting, legal fees, and more, without actually finding out if the idea is viable in your area or region. Imagine rushing off to get a new business certificate and setting up an LLC for every new idea that comes to you? It's not necessary. Go ahead and start your business and make some money, and then figure out your priorities. You may change the business concept, logo, name, and approach more than once in the first six months before you settle on a direction so who wants to have two outdated $350 logos.

The other important aspect of actual sales and revenues is that you will start to gain significant financial credibility, especially if this is your first time striking out on your own. Your bank, credit union, and other lenders are more likely to extend lines of credit and favorable terms based on the fact that your new venture has sales, customers, and clients.

Step Four - Roles

DEFINE Roles Among All The
Principals.

If you started your company by
yourself, you this might think this
chapter doesn't apply to you. But the
minute you grow, even a little bit, and
you take on some help, and then it will.

But for co-founders, partners, and
teams of "principals" that start
companies together, this step is critical.
For example, if two or three people
decide to start a company or business
together, the division of labor needs
some immediate discussion and
planning. Sometimes co-founders join
up because one has an idea but needs
other for implementation. But it's also

possible that a designer/inventor/ technologist developed a product and wanted to continue to focus on the tech side, finding partners to handle company management or sales.

[Image: folder-309052.png]

Here's an example for a three-person partnership:

- Principal/Co-Owner/Founder #1 would manage all the day-to-day operations and oversee hiring
- Principal/Co-Owner/Founder #2 would manage all the sales
- Principal/Co-Owner/Founder #3 would manage all the technology/ programming, etc

Seriously, decide early and discuss often the division of labor among the founders and partners. It's a good way to keep the company in a positive place for as long as possible. By then, money will be coming in, and you'll likely hire any help you need to grow, and all original partners can continue with their strengths and interests. Where it becomes a problem is if one person is actually building something -- round the clock -- and his or her equal partner is barely doing anything comparable to help the business, then hard feelings or a renegotiation might be in order.

Step Five - Tools

STAY Organized For Growth - Use
Modern Tools.

If you plan to run a business --
especially as a "solopreneur," it's easy to
get overwhelmed by all the 'moving
parts' of your business. If you have sales
and billing, shipping and receiving,
third-party suppliers, and general
accounting of revenues, accounting, and
expenses, it gets complicated fast -- even
well before it's a big business.

One of my small, side-businesses
got so cumbersome quickly that I almost
closed it down. But after catching my
breath, I realized that what was missing
was MORE organization. That side
business is now completely organized on

Google Drive (online spreadsheets, and shareable cloud document storage), Evernote (online files with tag system) and Asana (team collaboration platform).

I'm very passionate about using the right tools, although they can be a crutch. If you're a brand new wedding photographer with a great sense of framing, context, light, storytelling and have a good eye -- you shouldn't need a $4000 camera to launch your business. You can't use a pocket digital or iPhone, but you certainly shouldn't expect to start your company with high-end professional equipment. Maybe you bootstrap a few seasons of work and trade up to better gear (used!) every couple years!

That said, I knew a tech guy who created a powerful software tool that people kept buying and returning. It was very frustrating to him. When I did a little digging, I found that he never posted any free access screen-capture videos showing customers exactly how the product works and what to expect when they install it. When he described it to me, his passion and enthusiasm for the program are immediately apparent, so not having videos like these is probably also costing him sales.

He said that screen capture software like Camtasia, Screenflow, and others weren't a priority for his business because he was planning to buy finance and accounting software and buying some needed office equipment. But even so, there are cheaper (and free!)

alternatives to those screen-capture tools which would help him make videos satisfying the curiosity of customers who might buy his software only to return it, and to make additional sales by capturing the founder's enthusiasm.

Whether it's inventory management software, barcode scanners, specialty printers, or the right high-performance studio headphones, understand what your 'bottlenecks' are for growth -- what's slowing you down -- and find the modern tool that solves or bypasses that issue.

Step Six - The List

BUILD A List - Your Contacts, Customers, Suppliers, and Sub-Contractors -- Keep Everyone Happy, And The 'Reviews' Of Your Business Will Be Positive.

As you start your new company, it's more than customers that matter. You're building a major network of contacts. These can be leads, prospects, and potential customers, but your list can also include suppliers, subcontractors, and business development contacts. I would almost go so far as to say build a company-specific database, but you get what I mean.

The life-blood of your business is your customers, clients, and the people you work with inside and outside of your company. What you want is to over-deliver with your product or service to every one of your paying customers. If you figure out what your customers like about your product or service, it helps you develop new offerings. And it can also help you generate important marketing copy for ads, social media, and web listings.

If you have one happy customer, you should know how to reach them. You need to build a relationship of communication, even solicit their input on company offerings.

If you have a great supplier or sub-contractor, then always build a solid relationship with those people. You'll find that they will bring new ideas and opportunities to you based on their unique perspective to your business.

[Image: mail-793081.png]

Always build your lists and develop your company contacts and you'll encourage referrals. It might be a positive relationship with a business lawyer that turns into a referral for new customers. It could be a sub-contractor you hire who tells others to visit your website. Often a happy customer leaves great feedback for you online, re-posts your links online (Facebook, Twitter, Pinterest, Yelp, etc.), and refers you to others. That social proof is very valuable and leads to sales.

If you need new customers, and you were considering some form of advertising (direct mail, display, sponsorship, or PPC), then why not consider a referral (or affiliate) program for your company. Even my tax accountant offers a $30 rebate to any current client who refers a new client. It's easy to do. Offer a gift or rebate ($25 for example) or a percentage of cash back to customers who refer their friends or relatives. A referral program can be launched with a simple postcard or email that announces a "$25 Amazon or Apple iTunes Gift Card for Customers who refer new customers."

Some small businesses don't use outside workers, but if you do you might run into the problem that a friend of mine encountered. He launched an entertainment agency and needed to use subcontractors to fulfill each service. But he knew the field well, so he had a core

group of musicians, bands, singer/
guitarists, magicians, balloon artists,
etc., ready when he launched. But since
he wanted only to send the best
performers, it took him a while to
qualify his list. He spent an entire winter
collecting names, credentials, and
recordings from well-qualified violinists,
cellists, and other classical musicians so
that he could offer wedding ceremony
music in the spring and summer. It paid
off. And since there are multiple
weddings each weekend, and other
gigging conflicts, he made sure that he
had names of at least several 'approved'
musicians in each category. (The last
part was easy because at least one of the
other experienced, professional
musicians was able to vouch for others
without a formal audition process.)

Step Seven - Growth

DON'T Grow Too Fast.

For some of you this is a very valuable lesson: Keep a realistic eye on growth. It sounds very simple but is quite important. What happens if you start to get orders or clients so quickly that you completely run out of space, over-work all your employees, and bog down your accounting infrastructure? Well, then you'll have to grow or expand your operations. It happens, and it's a good thing. It's obviously what we want when we start our businesses. We want them to grow so well that they become self-sustaining growth engines and hopefully our main source of income for our family for years. In a perfect world, I'd also happily employ some friends, relatives, and other professionals and enjoy the fact that my business idea helps people pay their mortgages, enjoy their lives and put their kids through college.

But the mistake that many small business owners make is that if they happen to get an unexpected rush of new clients, new work, or new orders, they immediately assume a tidal wave is coming, and they upgrade everything. Do you honestly need to move into a much larger office just because you got five new clients? For those entrepreneurs working out of their garage or even a home office, just because a few more sales are coming through, should you upgrade to leasing commercial space? The timing of this decision is critical to the long-term success of your business. (Hint: Holding off on the move can increase the chances of long-term success of your business.)

Do you need to update to a new payroll system or bookkeeping subscription just because you have 20% more activity each month? Be very cautious and conservative about spikes in income, revenue, customers, opportunities, and more because some retained earnings and controlled spending can help you weather a tough winter when other companies might have to fold.

You want your company to flourish, but don't make rookie mistakes by assuming that you're growth is through the roof. Decide now to grow slow and steady, and then you're more likely to be in this for the long haul.

Your Action Plan

First off -- stay positive! Yes, you can do this. So to make this a very simple action plan, let's review the seven steps for starting fast. You'll find that this information in mind at every stage keeps you focused on the right things from the very beginning. Unless you're starting your side-business as a hobby, it's important to plan for success by avoiding these obvious pitfalls. This action plan will get you started fast, help you stay focused in the first six months to a year of business, and will help you start thinking about your long-term plan for growth. Best of luck with your new business!

Step One: Actually Launch.

Step Two: Realize That Your Website And Online Presence Is Not Your Business - Represent Yourself.

Step Three: Concentrate On The Money Coming In - Booking Work, Sales, Revenues, Cash Flow.

Step Four: Define Roles Among Principals.

Step Five: Stay Organized For Growth - Use Modern Tools.

Step Six: Build A List - Contacts, Customers, Suppliers, Sub-Contractors -- Keep Everyone Happy, And The 'Reviews' Of Your Business Will Be Positive.

Step Seven: Don't Grow Too Fast.

BONUS ROUND

Six More Steps to "TurboStart" Your Business

So I know that if you are reading this book, it means that you are thinking about starting -- or have already started -- your own small business. In today's economy, that may be one of the smartest moves you have ever made. The good news is that it has never been easier to start your own business, and create something that can support you full time. If you are not ready to take that plunge just yet, you can do something in your spare time, and just create a sideline business to supplement your income.

What's the best business for you to start? Only you know that. You should do something that you are good at, and something that you enjoy, because the hours likely will be long as you establish your business. If you like what you do, it won't be work. You can create an extra income stream for yourself, and have fun doing it. The following six bonus steps are designed to help you even more...

BONUS One: You are never too small to use "OPM."

What is OPM? It stands for "Other People's Money." And what do all of the best businesses in the world have in common? They have all used plenty of OPM to get started. If you're an entrepreneur, you have two key constraints on your ability to succeed. The first is your time, and the second is your money. After you've paid your living expenses each month, it can be very difficult to accumulate the excess capital that you need to start your own business. The good news is that you don't have to.

The world is awash in money. Banks, pension funds, and insurance companies have billions – even trillions- to invest, and they need to put those funds to productive use just as badly as you need money to get started. The world is not short of capital- it is short of good ideas like yours.

But even better, there are people who will give you money for free. Yes, for free. The crowd-funding phenomenon is still in its infancy, but the world of finance has never seen anything like it. On sites like Kickstarter, Gofundme, and Indiegogo, complete strangers will give you all the money you need to start your business. For free. If you ever find a better deal than that, please call and let me know!

BONUS Two: *Stay Asset Light*

The best businesses in the world have another thing in common. They are all asset-light. Your business should be too. Better yet, your business should have no assets at all.

What are assets? Put simply, they are the tools your business uses to make money. In the "old economy," assets were heavy, capital-intensive things like machinery and vehicles and real estate. In the information economy, assets were things like patents and computer code. But your business should only have one asset: the one that occupies the space between your ears.

Your brain should be the only asset your business "owns." Everything else should be outsourced, if possible. And with the web, you can do just that. There is an entire world of talent literally at your fingertips. With a few strokes of the keyboard on sites like Fiverr, Elance, and Freelancer.com, you can hire computer programmers in Asia, marketing experts in Latin America, and graphic designers in Eastern Europe. You can create your entire business virtually, with virtual assistants (Vas) -- and do it virtually overnight. And the whole process will probably cost you less than taking on even a part-time employee.

BONUS Three: *The "pre-launch" is the new launch*

No matter what business you create, there is going to be a lag between when you launch the business and when the revenues start rolling in. Whether it is one month or six months, you will be stuck in the economic doldrums for a while as you wait for your hard work to gain traction in the marketplace. This is an especially dangerous time for your financial well-being. You've probably already spent some money to get your business started. You need to get that money back in your pocket as quickly as possible (and have it bring its friends, too!)

How can you minimize the time you spend in these economic flatlands? Simple: by pre-launching your business. When the big pieces of your business are in place, you should have an idea about approximately when you will "go live." Don't wait passively for this date to roll around. Begin actively pre-selling your business. Create anticipation for your launch date with blog posts, social media pages, videos, and tweets. Generate buzz with press releases and online interviews. Better yet, generate actual money by pre-selling your product. Offer a discount now to those people who order your product or service before its official launch date. Get the orders coming in the door before the product launches, and you have a recipe for success.

BONUS Four: *Marketing, marketing, marketing*

You can have the best business in the world, but without proper marketing you are doomed to fail. The good news is that it doesn't have to be that way. It has never been easier to market your business. But you have to go about it the right way. Otherwise, you will just be wasting your hard-earned dollars on advertising that has no effect -- the proverbial tree falling in the woods that nobody hears.

It hardly seems fair, does it? If you make a fool out of yourself at a party, the internet will distribute the incident far and wide, and your infamy will live forever. But if you create the best product or service ever, the internet hardly seems to notice. Without proper marketing, your business will disappear without a trace. How do you make your business stand out from the online crowd? By finding the right medium for advertising your business- *and measuring it.*

Using some of the same tools mentioned above, you can find any advertising for your business- be it Facebook posts, blog mentions, tweets, and even radio. Advertising today is so easy, and so inexpensive, that you might be tempted to use a shotgun approach. After all, you want to get the word out to as many people as quickly as possible, right?

How do you start? Try one form of advertising at a time -- sending out paid tweets, targeted FB ads, or paying for a couple radio commercials or display ads in your area -- and then measure the impact of that single effort. Afterward, always check your page hits, analytics, or sales rankings, and then any pre-orders a day or two after each marketing push. Did it work? You need to measure the impact of each effort. If you have a dozen strategies going on at once, you won't know which one generates the results, and you'll waste money if you need to repeat the process.

This is also a great strategy to run during your pre-launch period. You get to tinker with your advertising mix while the stakes are lower before you even launch. Use the next month or two wisely to find out exactly what type of advertising has the most impact on your business. That way, when you are ready to go live, you can dump all your resources into those ad strategies and hit the ground running.

Bonus Five: *Own Your Customer Relationships*

Did you ever wonder why every product you buy seems to come with a warranty card that you are supposed to fill out and send back to the manufacturer? Hint: it has nothing to do with a warranty. Since the dawn of the advertising age, the holy grail that all manufacturers have pursued is direct contact with the customer. You should have that, too.

Make it easy for your customer to get in touch with you in any format they choose. Set up pages on LinkedIn, Twitter, Instagram, YouTube, and Facebook. Remember, you're not just trying to sell your customer on your current business products or services. In time, you will be selling them your future products and services as well. Create your list of email contacts that will enable you to reach all of your customers now and in the future.

Bonus Six: *Manage your online reputation*

Do you remember that old joke that goes "On the internet, nobody knows that you are a dog?" It's funny, but it's not true. On the internet, everybody knows if you are a dog. Review sites like Yelp and Tripadvisor make sure of it.

Everybody knows that customers will Google you long before they buy your product or service. And if they get a sense of bad vibes on the internet, forget it- the deal is off. Your online reputation is golden.

You can protect this reputation by setting up a Google alert for any keyword associated with your business. Read your online reviews regularly. If there is one that is particularly cutting, you should respond to it in written form. But don't try to fight fire with fire.

Always take the high road. If an "attack dog" review is met with a measured and thoughtful response, it will do more than neutralize the bad review. It might turn public opinion in your favor. And if a bad review is really over the line -- a harmful, slanderous, or personal attack -- consider contacting the website's service provider, and ask that it be deleted entirely.

There is one other technique that you can use to protect your online reputation. And it begins long before the customer buys your product or service. The technique is a simple one, and it goes like this: don't do business with "unreasonable" people. That's right. You should screen your customers just as carefully as your customers screen you. When someone inquires about your product or service, be on the lookout for inflammatory words or unjust behavior that sends up a red flag. If they come across as overly demanding, bullying, or intimidating -- perhaps you should drop the contact. Tell them that you are fully booked this week, and next week as well. Avoiding doing business with irrational people has another side benefit. It frees up your time and energy to do what you are supposed to be doing: providing a great product or service to customers who appreciate it. And that, at the end of the day, is the way to ensure that your online reputation stays golden.

So there you have it! These simple steps will ensure that your business launches as quickly and effectively as possible. The time to take charge of your financial well-being is now. And the person to take charge of it is you. Don't wait a minute longer to unlock your inner entrepreneur. Go launch and good luck!

Your Opinion

If you've enjoyed reading this short but hopefully helpful book, it would be great if you would help others find it as well. **LEND** it, **RECOMMEND** it, or **REVIEW** it.

The Seven Step Rocket Start-Up Plan: Your Hard Truth Cheat Sheet for Starting Your Own Successful Small Business

About the Author

Alan Kerrman is an individual investor and small business owner who lives near Boston, Massachusetts, USA. He is NOT a finance professional and is NOT a registered investment advisor, but an enthusiastic and motivated retail trader, investor, writer, entrepreneur, and full-time educator. He wants to succeed with his money and wants to help you succeed with yours by sharing what he's learned about finance, business, and investing along the way. He lives in an old New England house with his wife and daughter.

Other books by Alan Kerrman:

Trading Options on Tech Stocks

Investing in DRIPs

Published by Notable Media.

Author's Note

I've been blogging and ghostwriting

about a lot of this stuff for years, so it's

nice to publish a couple short books

sharing my thoughts and strategies! I

continue to learn, want always to

provide great value and help others,

and add to my growing collection of

books and ebooks -- it makes my wifey

and daughter proud. Thanks for

reading! And for those people who pre

ordered the book, you gave me

additional hope and purpose as I was

writing, so thank you! -- All best, A.K.

◇◇◇

Please consider leaving a review of this book, and thank you again for reading this!

Please visit http://

www.dripinvestingplans.com